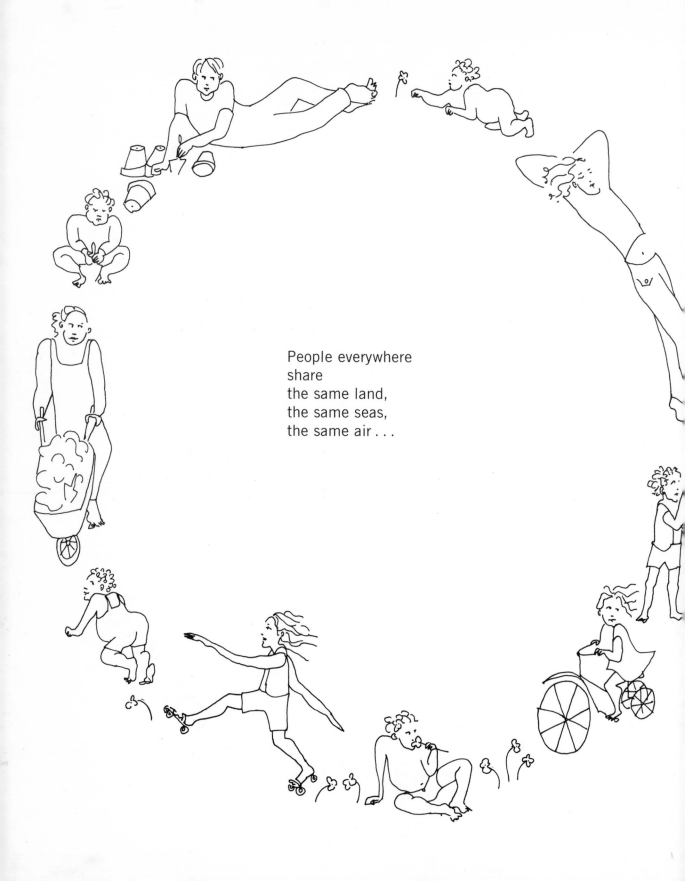

People everywhere
share
the same land,
the same seas,
the same air . . .

SAVE THE EARTH!

by Betty Miles   illustrated by Claire A. Nivola

An Ecology Handbook for Kids

Alfred A. Knopf, New York

THIS IS A BORZOI BOOK PUBLISHED BY ALFRED A. KNOPF, INC.

Copyright © 1974 by Betty Miles   All rights reserved under International and Pan-American Copyright Conventions. Published in the United States by
Alfred A. Knopf, Inc., New York, and simultaneously in Canada by Random House of Canada Limited, Toronto. Distributed by Random House, Inc., New York.
Library of Congress Cataloging in Publication Data   Miles, Betty. Save the earth!   SUMMARY: Discusses the ecological problems of land, air, and water pollution
in the world today. Includes projects that illustrate these problems and possible solutions to them.   1. Ecology – Juvenile literature. 2. Conservation of natural
resources – Juvenile literature. [1. Ecology. 2. Conservation of natural resources] I. Nivola, Claire, illus. II. TITLE.   QH541.14.M54 333.7'2 73-15116
ISBN 0-394-82658-2   ISBN 0-394-92658-7 (lib. bdg.)   Manufactured in the United States of America

Designed by Claire A. Nivola

With special acknowledgement to Pat Ross and Frances Foster
for creative editorial guidance and ongoing support.

Table of

Contents

Introduction

People share one earth: the land, the seas and the thin layer of air around them, warmed by the sun.

The earth is always changing. The land shifts, air and water flow in changing patterns. Plants and animals and people live and grow and die. These are natural changes.

People change the earth, too. More and more people, with more and more wants and more complicated problems live on the earth, use up parts of it, study it, spoil it, or learn to understand it.

Ecology is the study of the changes, and the connections on the earth.

Everything that happens on the earth is connected. The height of a mountain is connected to how much rain falls from the air flowing over it. The amount of rain is connected to what kinds of plants grow in the valleys, what kinds of animals live among the plants, and the way of life of the people who farm the valleys, build houses and schools and shopping centers and cities. The way people think about their earth is connected to the ways they live on it and use it.

When people poison the fish in the oceans, cut down great forests, fill the air with dirt and smoke and gases, they spoil the earth.

When people work to clean up the water and the air, to preserve wild lands, plant trees and plan cities, learn to care about ecology, they begin to save the whole earth.

Every person can help to save the earth. You can.

This book shows some of the earth's problems, and tells about ways that people have started to solve them.

Learning about the problems, and inventing solutions, is one step toward saving the earth.

The next step is working hard to make the solutions happen. This book gives you suggestions about things you can do that will really make a difference.

It is terrible to know that land on the earth is stripped and torn apart, air is filled with poisons, and water is fouled. It is exciting to know that many people care enough about the earth to fight for it. Right now, people across this country are working for ecology. You can work with them. You and your friends can become part of the most important movement on earth: the movement to save it.

Betty Miles

Land

For millions of years the land was wild: desert, jungle, mountain, plain. There was land enough for everyone.

People and the Land

Now, four billion (4,000,000,000) people live on the land. Each one of them needs a place to live, and space to move about.

People need land for farms, houses, schools, stores, factories, hospitals, parking lots, offices. They build towns on the land, and roads from one town to another. As more and more people are born, more and more land is needed.

In some places, cities cover the land.

People need materials to build with. They cut down trees to make lumber. People need newspapers and wrappings. They cut down more trees. Sometimes whole forests are cut down, leaving the land bare and unprotected—abused.

People need power to make machines work. They mine the land for coal to make electricity. To get coal cheaply and quickly, people strip coal from the surface of the land, leaving it cut up and raw.

People need land for growing food and raising animals. Plants need rich soil to grow. But when the land is planted with the same crops over and over, some minerals in the soil are used up, and the plants thin out.

When animals graze on the land for too long, they use up the grass and leave the land bare. When there is no grass, there are no roots to draw rain into the ground, and the rich topsoil can be swept off by the rain, and blown away by the wind. Dry land is wasted land, lying cracked and barren under the sun. Land that is eroded like this will be wasted for a long time.

People need the land. People need space to move in and a place to live. They need energy, food, building materials. They need cities with trees and parks and play space, and they need the beauty of open land.

People can waste the land, or they can plan to save it.

Everywhere Is Somewhere

When you throw away a glass bottle,

or an aluminum can,

you have not really thrown it "away."

A broken piece of glass on a path

is somewhere —

it is *there.*

When you walk along that path,

even years later,

you can step on the glass and cut yourself.

A can thrown behind a rock is there,

even if you can't see it.

It will go on being there

for hundreds and hundreds of years.

On the land,

everywhere is somewhere.

Nowhere is "away."

Every Person's Trash

Every day, people make millions of pounds of garbage and trash in their homes and at work. Much of this waste goes onto the land. Some of it is biodegradable—it decays naturally and becomes part of the soil again. But some of the waste—like soda bottles, plastic containers, and beer cans—stays on the surface of the land for a long, long time.

Enough waste is thrown out each day in the United States to make a five-pound pile for every single person in the country, every day of the year.

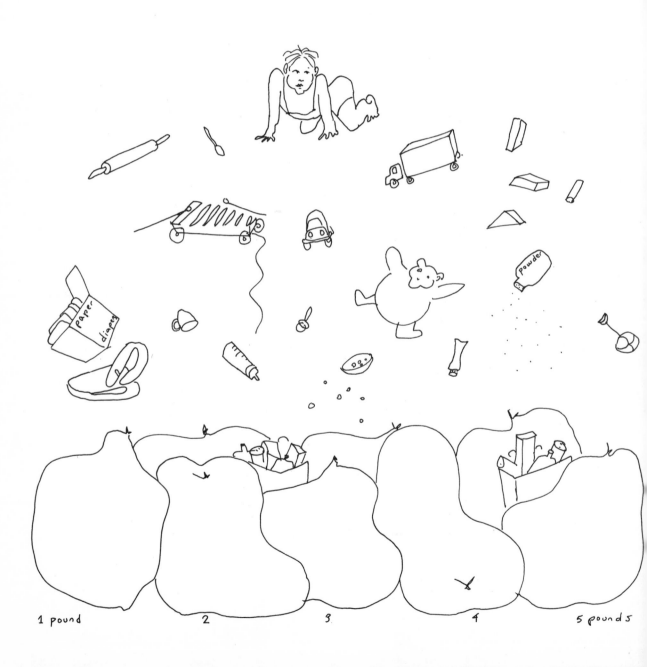

1 pound   2   3   4   5 pounds

How the Trash Pile Grows

Buy it,

try it,

throw the trash away!

Take it,

break it,

throw the trash away!

Get it,

use it,

finish it,

lose it.

Wear it,

tear it,

throw the trash away!

Soda pop,

box top,

once you start

you can't stop.

Buy it,

show it,

nothing left but throw it:

Throw the trash away!

(Oh, no — where is "away"?)

bait

Taking Action—The Story of Mount Trashmore

A few years ago, Virginia Beach, Virginia, was a flat, sandy city near the ocean.

Like every other city, Virginia Beach had a problem: people kept making garbage and trash, and the city kept having to get rid of it. It cost the city a lot of money to collect it, dump it, burn it, collect it again, dump it, burn it, and so on.

A dump full of burning waste looks ugly and smells bad. Its smoke pollutes the air. Rats are attracted to the garbage. Not all the waste burns up. The dump makes an ugly, useless scar on the land.

Some people in Virginia Beach had an idea. "Let's do something useful with our trash. Let's pile it up, cover it with dirt, and make ourselves a mountain."

It costs money to try something new and to find out whether it works. The United States government gave Virginia Beach money for the experiment. If it worked in Virginia Beach, it might work in other places.

Virginia Beach already had a town dump, and this is where they decided to put the mountain. Swampy land was drained and flattened, and roads to the area were built.

Then workmen spread trash out over the dump. This trash was everything that people in Virginia Beach threw away. Not just food garbage, like orange peels and watermelon rinds and coffee grounds. Not just paper trash like boxes and newspapers and paper bags. This was *all* the waste: buckets and tires and broken stoves, car parts and coat hangers and old toys and table legs. Everything.

On top of this trash they dumped a layer of dirt about twenty inches thick. A machine called a compacter rolled over

the dump, packing the trash and the dirt so tightly together that it became a solid block — the first layer of the mountain.

Of course, more trash kept coming, and the mountain kept growing. Every day loads of trash were dumped, spread out covered with soil, compacted. The mountain grew higher.

After five years, 640,000 tons of trash, and one million dollars, the mountain was finished. It was 800 feet long, 300 feet wide and 68 feet high with a broad flat top — not much of a mountain, but something special in flat Virginia Beach.

The finished mountain stood there with no name until someone came along and

called it "Mount Trashmore." The name stuck. When government mapmakers put it on the map, they printed "Mount Trashmore" on it. That made it official.

Grass now grows on Mount Trashmore. Soon there will be bicycle trails, riding paths, tennis courts, and an outdoor theater. There will be boating and fishing on a man-made lake nearby.

What did Virginia Beach get from the Mount Trashmore experiment? It got rid of its waste for two dollars a ton, instead of paying seven to thirteen dollars a ton to burn it. It got rid of an ugly dump. It got rid of air pollution from burning waste. It got rid of rats.

It also got visitors, who came from cities all over the world to learn about Mount Trashmore. And one winter, when a surprise snow fell, Virginia Beach got its very first ski slope — the side of Mount Trashmore.

Of course, people in Virginia Beach are still making garbage and trash — and the city still has to get rid of it. So they are beginning to build a new mountain, which will grow from the garbage and trash of the next twenty years. And then?

Saving the Land

People can save the land in many ways.

They can plan parks and playgrounds in cities and in suburbs.

People can work to enforce existing laws which were made to protect the wilderness—to keep some wild land forever wild. Then animals can live in peace among the trees and plants that give them shelter, and people can discover what it is like to move quietly through deep forests.

People can farm the land carefully: plant crops that enrich the soil; cover bare ground with plants and trees to hold the topsoil in place; plow the ground in level curves to hold the rain water and keep it from running off, carrying the rich topsoil with it.

People don't have to spoil the land when they build houses. People can plan developments carefully —

like this   instead of this.

They can leave the woods undisturbed. Open space can be saved for everyone to use, and for its natural beauty.

People can plant flowers to make the land look bright. They can plant trees to keep the land from washing away, keep the air fresh and cool, make a place for birds to live, and give a thick green shade.

Projects about Land

People can use things over and over — recycle.

Old newspapers can be used to make new paper; old metal can be used in making new metal; old bottles can make new glass.

If re-useable trash is recycled, the land can be saved from ugly dumps.

There are useful ways to get rid of waste: compacting it into building materials, using it for landfill, or burning it in such a way that the heat from the burning can be used as energy.

Every machine uses energy and our sources of energy are limited, so people can try to cut down their use of machines, like electric pencil sharpeners and electric can openers, that are not absolutely necessary.

People can save energy for their most basic needs, like heat and light. And people can use sources of energy — the sun and the winds, shifting tides and underground hot springs — that can be developed in ways that do not spoil the environment.

Saving the land now is a step toward saving the land for the future; for children to come and their children's children.

1. Planning New Town

a one-hour project

This land is going to be developed for New Town. Three hundred people will live here. There will be people of all ages, from new babies to very old people.

New Town will have one-family houses, apartment houses, an elementary school, some stores, a community center and a town office building. Many people who will live here work in Old Town, which is connected to New Town by a highway.

You can try out different plans for New Town. Use pennies for houses, nickels for apartment houses, quarters for larger buildings. Use toothpicks for roads. Move them around while you think about these questions:

How can the land be divided into enough space for living without cutting down all of the trees on it now?

How can people get from one house to another, and to school and the store, without having to cross busy streets? Without having to use a car for every trip?

How much space could be saved for open land? For swimming? A playground and park for children and old people? Or other things you think of.

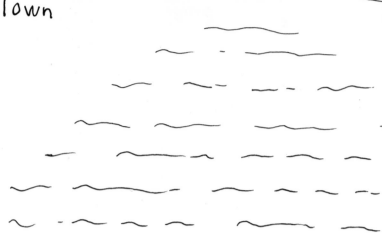

meadows

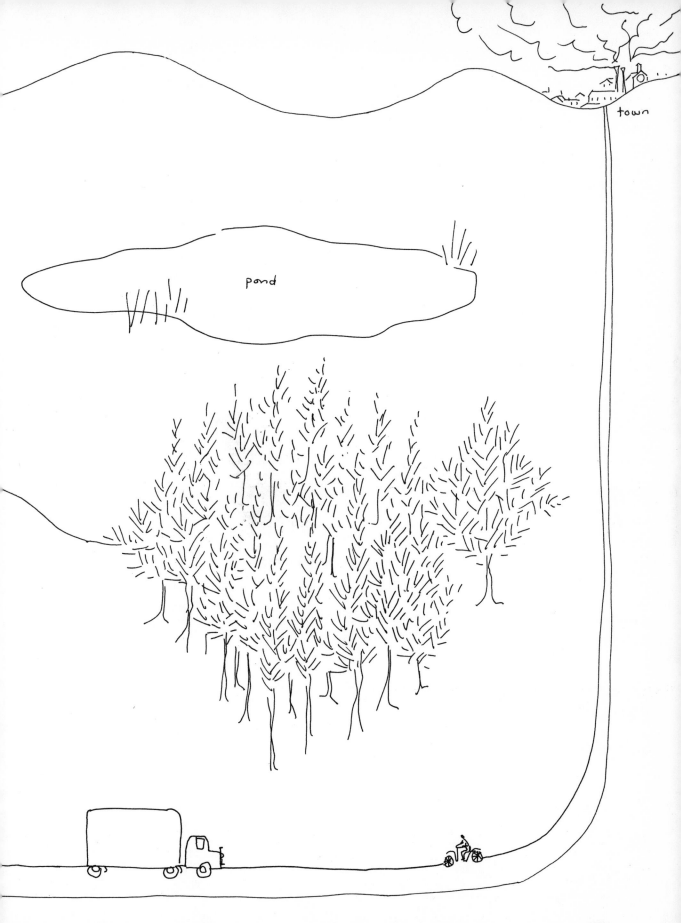

town

pond

2. "No Bag, Please"

a one-hour project

Everyone knows that when you save paper, you save some trees that would have to be cut down to make new paper.

Everyone knows this. But you can find out how hard it is for people to get used to saving paper.

Try this project when you are going shopping. Take a big shopping bag with you to put things in. When you pay for something watch carefully. Does the person at the counter start to put it in a bag for you?

If this happens, say "I don't need a bag, thanks."

Then see how the store person acts. Surprised? Pleased? A little bit angry? Confused?

Then see how you feel. Ordinary? Embarrassed? Good?

It is sometimes easier to try new ways if you can get other people to try them with you. Maybe a friend or two from school would try the "no bag, please" experiment with you.

3. Unwrapping and Unwrapping

a 15-minute project

Try this when someone in your family has come home from the store with lots of groceries.

Put an empty wastebasket near the table. Now start unwrapping the groceries before you put them away.

Put every piece of wrapping in the wastebasket:

cardboard boxes

ice cream bags plastic bags paper bags

cardboard cartons

Did you collect a wastebasket full of wrappings? Do you think all those wrappings were really necessary?

4. People Space

a one-hour project

This project is for four different classes in your school (or four different groups in your own class).

First, with your own group, choose a section of the playground that you think is big enough to play in comfortably. Mark it off with a chalk line, or with a rope.

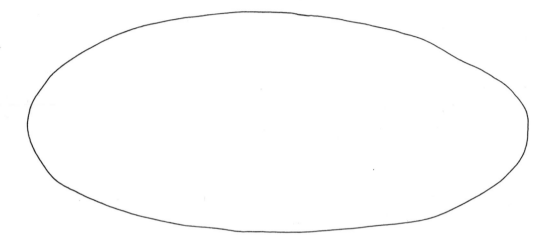

Then ask another group to come and play with you in your space.

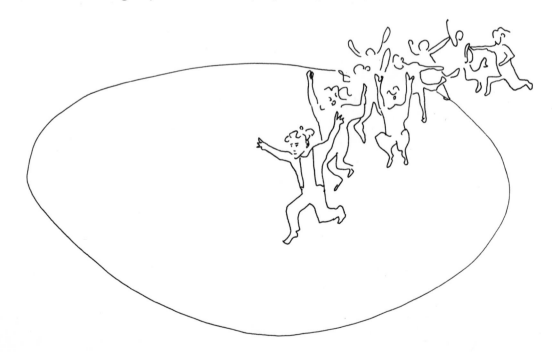

Now ask another group to come.

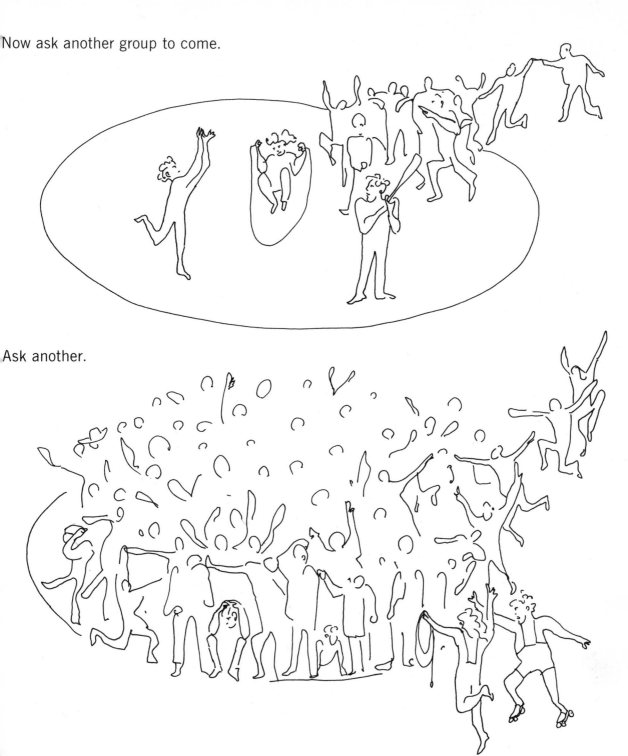

Ask another.

What happened?
Did you have to change the way you played?
Did you like having so many people in your space?
Did it get noisy?
What about people's tempers?

5. How Many Grandchildren?

This diagram shows the number of great-grandchildren you would have if you had two children, and those children each had two children, and those children each had two children.

This page begins to show what could happen if you had *four* children. Take a large piece of paper and make a diagram showing how many children there would be if each had four children and each of *them* had four children.

In a very small way, these diagrams show how every family's size makes a difference in the number of people in the future.

Air

A thin layer of air — the air all plants and animals need for life — lies over the land. Sunlight and cloud, rain and snow, storm and fog and all weather move over the land as the air shifts and changes.

People and the Air

Long ago, the air carried only natural things: moisture that turned into rain; dust blown up by the wind; pollen and seeds from plants. Birds flew through the clear air. There was smoke from people's fires, but not enough to darken the sky.

Now the air around us is sometimes thick with pollution. Dirt and soot, poisoned fumes and gasses are bad for everyone who breathes them. Polluted air makes people sick when it carries poisons into their bodies, or fills their lungs with soot or factory dust. Polluted air can kill plants. Polluted air hangs over many towns and cities and darkens whole valleys.

The needs and wants of billions of people often lead to air pollution. People need electricity, and the coal that is burned to make it pours smoke into the air. People need the factories that make things to wear and use and enjoy.

But factories often send
smoke, or particles of dust or
soot or dangerous fumes and
chemicals into the air.

People need cars. In this country, some
families have two cars, or even three.
Every car that moves pollutes the air
when it burns gasoline and sends fumes
out of the exhaust pipe. The air is full
of the enormous pollution of cars and
trucks and busses — and the pollution of
airplanes streaking fumes across the sky.

People need to get rid of their waste.
In many places, people still just dump
trash on the land, and burn it. Clouds of
soot pour into the air.

The bitter smell of burning rubbish, the
sharp fumes of chemicals, the sickly
smell of gasses — all of these smells are a
kind of air pollution.

Another kind of pollution comes from noise. The sounds of people and machines fill the air of busy cities, and the quiet country is sometimes noisy with the sounds of jet planes and snowmobiles, power saws and bulldozers.

People get used to noise pollution, and learn to shut sound out of their minds. But steady noise can make people lose sleep, have accidents, get exhausted, behave angrily, and even become deaf.

Noise pollution is measured in decibels. At zero decibels, a sound is so soft you can hardly hear it. At 180 decibels, noise can kill you.

Common Sounds in Decibels

10	rustling leaves
20	whispering
60	talking
70	vacuum cleaner; loud TV sound
80	SOUND DANGER BEGINS
90	heavy city traffic
100	a jet plane 1,000 feet away
110	jackhammer; snowmobile
115	a rock group, close to you
120	PAIN BEGINS
140	the eardrum can break

People need clear air. People can darken the air with smoke and dirt, fill it with unpleasant smells and crashing noise. People can spoil the air, or they can work to save it.

Everywhere Is Somewhere

When people spray poisons into the air

to kill plant-eating insects,

the insects may die

but the poison does not go away.

It stays, unseen, in the air.

And it falls, perhaps years later,

on other plants, and on the land.

When the rains come, some poisons wash off of plants

and run off the land

into ponds and lakes and rivers.

The poison is always somewhere.

It gets into water plants

and small water animals

and into the fish that eat them.

Birds of the air catch the poisoned fish,

or eat the poisoned insects,

and poison gets into the birds.

The poisoned birds lay eggs with soft eggshells.

No baby birds will come out of these eggs.

Some kinds of birds will never fly through the air again.

They are gone forever,

because of poisons in the air.

In the air, everywhere is somewhere.

Nowhere is away.

Every Person's Air

Every person alive uses 6,000 gallons of air a day, just breathing in and breathing out. The same air has been used over and over again by all the people on earth, for thousands of years.

6,000

5,000

4,000

3,000

2,000

1,000
gallons

Noisy Noise

Here,
there,
everywhere,
noisy noise
is in the air.

Buses rumbling,
people grumbling,
buildings tumbling.

Dogs yipping,
clippers clipping,
TV going,
mowers mowing.

Screech,
yell,
siren, bell,
crash,
shout—

Hey! Turn it down!
Cut it out!

Taking Action—
The Story of Pittsburgh and the Long Clean-Up

Cleaning up the air of a large city is not easy. It can take many years and cost huge amounts of money. But it can be done, and the people of the city of Pittsburgh are proving it.

More than a hundred years ago, people in Pittsburgh began to worry about their dirty air, filled with smoke from homes and factories, and from boats going up and down the river. One visitor said, "Pittsburgh is, without exception, the blackest place I ever saw. The city itself is buried in a dense cloud."

Another visitor said that Pittsburgh was "hell with the lid off."

Something had to be done to clean up Pittsburgh's air. The newspaper said so, people in government said so, ordinary citizens said so. And in 1895, the City of Pittsburgh passed one of the first smoke control laws in the United States.

But the law didn't help. Factories didn't obey it, and the city didn't enforce it. The city grew larger, more and more factories were built, and the air got worse.

The city passed new smoke control laws. But no one obeyed them, and no one enforced them. The air stayed dirty.

Law after law was passed but nothing changed. The city kept growing, and so did the amount of smoke in the air.

In the daytime, Pittsburgh looked like a twilight city. It was unpleasant to live there because of the polluted air.

People didn't like to walk in the city, because the smoke in the air made them cough and made their eyes hurt.

People didn't like to drive in the city,

because they could hardly see where they were going.

People didn't like to clean up the buildings in Pittsburgh, because they just got dirty again.

People didn't like to plant trees and flowers in the city, because they didn't grow well in the foul air.

They didn't like to work in Pittsburgh. Hard work in thick, dirty air made people tired and sick.

No one liked to look at the city. The city was ugly.

People made jokes about the air in Pittsburgh, but it wasn't funny.

The air in Pittsburgh got so bad that people couldn't stand it any more. Citizens began to demand clean air.

The newspapers called for stronger smoke control laws.

Gradually, Pittsburgh, and Allegheny County around it, began to change the things that made air pollution.

Houses began to use gas instead of coal for heating.

Engines and river boats no longer burned coal.

Many factories began to clean up their dirt *before* it went out the smokestacks.

The air began to clear up.

Finally, in 1969, a group of citizens in Pittsburgh formed the Group Against Smog and Pollution, or GASP. GASP grew into a powerful organization of 40,000 citizens, all of them working together to get clean air.

They learned the facts about air pollution.

They found out who the big polluters were.

They helped to write strong laws against pollution.

They learned how to bring polluters to court.

Members of GASP keep studying, talking, writing, and fighting for clean air. They have learned that laws against pollution are not enough—people must see that the laws are enforced. The slogan of GASP is:
Don't hold your breath . . . fight for it!

Today, Pittsburgh looks like this. The air over Pittsburgh is not free of pollution yet, but there was 10 percent less pollution in 1972 than in 1971. Many industries have changed or are changing to the cleaner ways of operation that can be arranged today with anti-pollution devices. Most industries realize that it is their responsibility to pay for their own clean-up.

Meanwhile, most citizens know that it is their responsibility to complain when they see a factory polluting the air. And government officials know it is their responsibility to investigate complaints. Fifteen patrol cars drive around the county, ready to check on polluters within 15 minutes of a citizen's complaint.

After one hundred years of smoke, the City of Pittsburgh is on the way to cleaner air. People, working together, can save the air.

Saving the Air

People can save the air in other ways.

Solving the problem of exhaust from cars and other vehicles is one of the most important ways to cut down air pollution.

Having all cars equipped with effective emission-control devices that clean up the exhaust of gasoline-powered engines will help; so will the use of smaller cars that burn less fuel. Developing electric cars should help even more.

But also people will have to use cars less. They can use car pools to carry several people instead of one.

There are ways to move more people with less pollution: moving sidewalks, mass-transit trains that go fast and quietly over or under cities; electric mini-buses that drive through town and suburbs picking up passengers.

And people can use bicycles more. Bicycles don't pollute the air, and they give pleasure to their riders.

People can demand more laws that control air pollution, and then see that the laws are kept.

People are finding new ways to get rid of waste, so that they do not pollute the air by burning it. When waste is buried, or compacted, or recycled, there is no smell; there are no fumes.

Some waste materials can be recycled for people to use, instead of being burned on dirty, foul-smelling dumps.

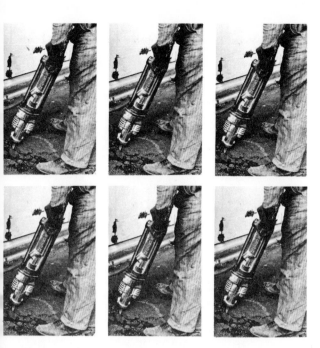

People can work to stop noise pollution: they can make laws to keep noise down, and make sure that people obey the laws.

And everyone can easily stop some kinds of noise.

It is easy to turn down the TV or the radio.

It is possible to get dogs to stop barking, and drivers to stop honking. It is also possible to make quieter machines.

People can work to save the air, to make it healthier and more pleasant now, and for their children, and their children's children.

Projects about Air

1. Catching Pollution

a 24-hour project

Spread a thin layer of vaseline on some pieces of cardboard, or small cards.

Put the cards outdoors in different places:

on your front step,

on a window sill, or taped to the outside of a window,

fastened to a tree, or to a building near a busy corner.

A day later, check your card Whatever is stuck to each ca is a record of one day's pollution in that place.

2. Car Exhaust

a 10-minute project

Put a white sock over the exhaust pipe of a car that has been parked for awhile so the pipe is cool. Ask the driver to turn the engine on for a minute, and then to turn it off.

Pull the sock off the exhaust pipe carefully (the pipe may be hot) and look inside it.

The pollution in the sock is just part of the pollution you breathe from one car's exhaust. (Some of it is invisible).

Think about all the pollution you breathe from car exhausts when you cross a busy street!

3. Pollution Detective

If you see a factory near you polluting the air with clouds of soot and smoke from its smokestacks, you can make a record of the pollution to prove it.

Every day for a week, at the same time of day, stand in exactly the same place, and take a photograph of the factory. Write down the day, the time and the place in your notebook. When your pictures are developed, you will have proof of pollution.

Now, find out what agency in your town or city is in charge of controlling air pollution and take your evidence of pollution to that agency.

4. The Quietest Place

a 15-minute project

Take a pencil and a piece of paper and go to the quietest place you know—a room in your house, or the library, or maybe some outdoor place.

Now, be very quiet yourself, and listen. What do you hear?

people whispering? footsteps? radio music? airplane noises? cars driving past? birds? barking dogs?

Write down every sound you hear, and see how long a list you have made.

Most "quiet" places have a steady hum of noise, but people get so used to it they don't really hear it unless they listen carefully.

In really noisy places, the noise is so loud you *have* to hear it. Having to listen to noise takes energy, and that's why noise can make you tired.

5. Smoking Without Cigarettes

a project to finish as fast as you can

This is a project to do when you can't help being in a closed room with many people who are smoking.

Breathe.
Pay attention to your eyes. Do they sting?
Pay attention to your throat. Does it feel sore?
Pay attention to your head. Does it ache?
Pay attention to your chest. Do you feel like coughing?
Do you feel a little bit faint and dizzy?

As soon as you can, go outside where no one is smoking.
Breathe deeply.
Can you feel the difference?

Water

Long ago, water ran bright and clear in streams and lakes, rivers and ponds; and the salt seas were clean.

People and the Water

Water falls onto the ground in rain, and runs off in streams or seeps deep into rivers under the earth. From all streams, underground or above it, water flows to the sea.

Warm air, thick with moisture, rises from the seas, cools off into clouds, and falls again onto the land as rain. The same water, over and over, travels through the air and onto the land. People today use the same water that their ancestors used and that their children and their children's children will use.

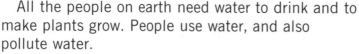

All the people on earth need water to drink and to make plants grow. People use water, and also pollute water.

People pollute water in many ways. For a long time, most people have used streams and rivers as a place to get rid of their sewage. Giant sewer pipes sometimes empty raw sewage into streams, carrying filth and disease to the water that will flow to another place. Small water plants feed on the sewage, and a slime of algae grows and spreads over polluted streams. Water plants and animals, and birds that live near the water, die.

Some factories pollute water when they empty their waste — dirt, paint, chemicals — into rivers. The waste can clog up streams and poison water plants, birds and fish.

Some factories, particularly power plants that use water to make energy, turn cool river water into hot water and send it back into the rivers. The hot water can kill water plants and fish for miles around the factory.

People build giant offshore drilling towers to take oil from beneath the water, and ship it across the seas in huge tankers. Oil from offshore drilling and from tanker accidents has spilled onto oceans and beaches, covering miles of water or miles of land with a thick layer of oil that kills birds and fish, pollutes the land and water, and costs millions of dollars to clean up.

For many years people have used the oceans as a giant dumping ground for all kinds of waste. Deadly waste poisons the seas.

Ugly dump heaps along river banks pollute and spoil the beauty of inland streams.

People can pollute water and waste it—or they can plan to clean it up and save it.

Everywhere Is Somewhere

When you rinse garbage down the drain of a sink,

or flush trash down the toilet,

It does not go away;

It goes somewhere.

Sewage and waste go into big pipes.

The pipes go into the river;

The river runs into a bigger river.

The big river flows to the sea.

Far, far away

In the middle of the ocean,

garbage and trash float on the sea water.

Pollution does not float away;

It floats somewhere.

And it will stay there,

floating and sinking under the sun,

for years and years.

When you rinse something down the drain,

It does not go away—

It goes somewhere.

In the water, everywhere is somewhere.

Every Person's Water

Enough water is used in homes, business, and government in the United States to add up to 150 gallons a day for every person who lives here!

150
100
75
50
25
Gallons

The Dirty Water Blues

Pure water gurgles

and splashes along

until pollution

flows into the song:

oil

tar,

paint

dye,

mud and muck

come splashing by.

Cans

jars,

bottles

cars.

Old shoes, old news —

that's the dirty water blues.

Sweet, fresh water

rolls away from this song,

while dirt and pollution

keep flowing along

and along,

and along...

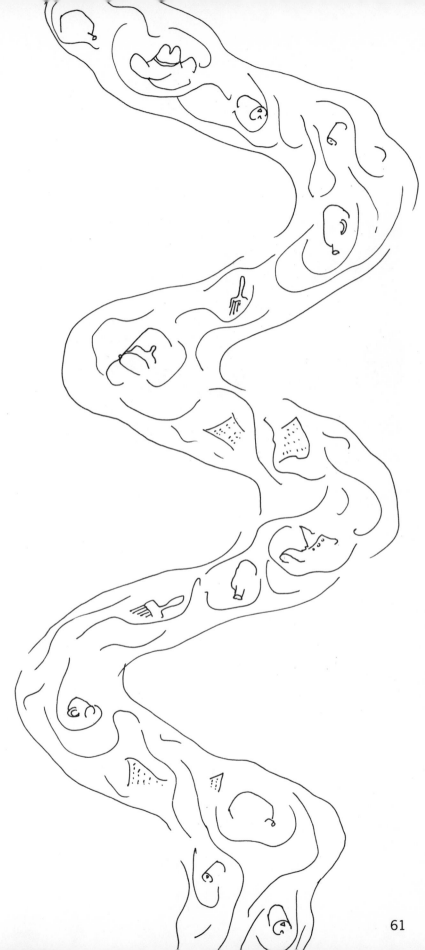

Taking Action—
The Story of the *Clearwater* and the Hudson River

Once, a long time ago, the Hudson River looked like this.

In those days, the river was so fresh, and so clean, the people could drink it, swim in it and eat the fish they caught in it.

The river was so beautiful, that people came from far away, just to look at it. Big boats and sloops sailed up and down the river, carrying passengers from New York to Albany.

Towns along the river grew. Factories were built to take advantage of the Hudson's water power. Oil and coal and stone and ice were sent by boat down the Hudson River to New York City.

And people dumped all their dirty water, their garbage, their sewage and their trash into the Hudson. They flushed it all down into the Hudson. People didn't know any better, then. The river was there, they thought, so why not use it?

By the time people began to realize they were spoiling the river, it was almost too late to clean it up.

People who had houses along the river said, "our waste can't make a difference. There's such a little bit of it."

People who owned factories said, "It would really cost us too much to clean up our waste."

People in town governments said nothing. They sent their towns' waste floating on down the river, for the people in the next town to worry about.

Nobody did anything and the Hudson River turned into a foul, polluted river.

People didn't swim in it anymore, unless they wanted to swim in sewage.

People didn't fish in it, because many kinds of fish just weren't there any more.

And many people didn't even want to take a close look at it. (In some places, the Hudson River looked like a giant toilet.)

Can the Hudson River run clear again?

Many people think so.

One group has built a boat to sail the Hudson and work to clean it up. The *Clearwater* looks like the Hudson River sloops of a hundred years ago, but it does new things.

People on the *Clearwater* sail up and down the Hudson with groups of school children from river towns. The children learn how to help sail the sloop. They also learn how to use scientific instruments to measure the amount of solids polluting the water, the temperature of the water, and the underwater noises that show what life there is on the river botton.

People who have sailed on the *Clearwater* learn to care about the Hudson River in a special way. Then they teach other people.

Sometimes the *Clearwater* ties up by a river town for a river festival. People come aboard the sloop and learn about the river—its history and its future. They learn how to work with others to catch polluters and bring them to court. They learn how to work for new and stronger laws against pollution. When people find out about the fight for clean water, they get excited and join the fight themselves.

The Hudson River is getting cleaner. There is more oxygen in the river today than there has been since the very early years of this century. Some kinds of fish that had almost disappeared are beginning to be found once again in the river. In many places, the dumps along the Hudson's shores are being cleaned up.

There is a long way to go. Meanwhile, the *Clearwater* sails up and down the Hudson reminding people that clear water is everyone's right.

As they sail, people on the sloop sing this song. Someday, the words will come true.

Bound to get Clear Water

Oh, little piece of shortcake, little piece of pie, to my heave a-way, to my

haul away, I'm gonna sail un-til I die. Bound to get clear water.

haul away you rolling king, to my heave away, to my haul away,

haul away and hear me sing. we're bound to get clear water.

Saving the Water

People can save the water in other ways.

There is an international law which makes it illegal to dump dangerous waste in the oceans. This law is a first step but it has to be enforced, and many more laws will have to be written to keep the oceans pure. Someday countries, like factories, will be responsible for cleaning all their waste before it flows into the oceans.

Water can be recycled over and over again. Sewage systems have been developed that return sewage wastes to the soil as fertilizer and return the water, pure and clean, to water pipes for drinking.

Factories can recycle water, using the same amount over and over again. Factories can clean waste from the water they have used before they let it run back into rivers.

People can plan for careful water use when they plan for good use of land. They can plant crops that hold the rain so that it seeps deep into the earth. They can plow small ridges in grazing land to catch and hold water so that it does not run off and take rich topsoil with it. They can protect the wetlands — the open marshes and swamps which are giant natural reservoirs of water.

People can work on economical ways to take salt out of sea water so that it can be used for drinking and for farming. They can take cool rich water from the ocean depths and use it to cool off power plants along the shore. This deep water, which is naturally rich in nutrients, can then be directed to nearby shallows where it will nourish fish and shellfish.

People can clean up the water by cleaning up stream and river banks and making sure that no one is allowed to dump trash there.

People can find out about the laws against polluters, and test water to learn whether the laws are being broken. They can find out how to make complaints against polluters, and how to bring them to court.

People need fresh water for life — and for pleasure. People can plan for careful water use, and learn to save clear water for everyone, now and in the future.

Projects about Water

1. Water Count
an all-day project

As soon as you get up in the morning, put a little notebook and a pencil in your pocket.

All day long, make a note *every time* you use some water.

Don't forget.

At the end of the day, see how long your list is. Are you surprised at how many different ways you have used water? How many gallons do you think you used? (Do you know that every flush of a toilet takes eight gallons of water?)

2. Catching Rain
an overnight project

When rain is predicted, put a pail outside your house to catch some of it.

After twenty-four hours, measure the depth of the water in the pail. The number of inches (or the part of an inch) you have measured is the rainfall rate for that day where you live.

If you have caught a lot of rainwater, save it to use later.

3. Tracking Water Pollution

an afternoon project

First, find some water near you.

If you live in the country, it might be a mountain brook, or a creek.

If you live in the suburbs, it might be a marsh, or a ditch by a roadside.

If you live in the city, it might be a river, or a lake in a park.

Take a walk along that water.

As you walk, write down all the pollution that you can see — trash, garbage, sewage, oil, chemical waste — and the place where you found it. (Of course you don't see all the pollution in water. Germs and many chemicals are invisible.)

When you get home, make a map of the water and the polluted places.

When you have a water pollution map, you can begin to track down the sources of pollution. It may be a factory that is dumping waste into a river; or it could be a picnic place where people throw away their paper plates. Whatever the source is, if you can find it and report it to the proper agency, you will have begun to clean up the water.

4. Catching a Leak

an overnight project

If you have a leaky faucet in your house, put a pail under it, to catch the drip. Leave the pail there overnight.

The next morning, see how much water ran out of that leak. When you find out, you may want to learn how to fix leaks so that you don't waste water in your house that way anymore.

5. Bath or Shower?

a 5-minute project

Which uses more water, a bath or a shower?

To find out, plug up the tub drain and take a shower.

Is the shower water you caught in the tub as deep as the baths you usually run?

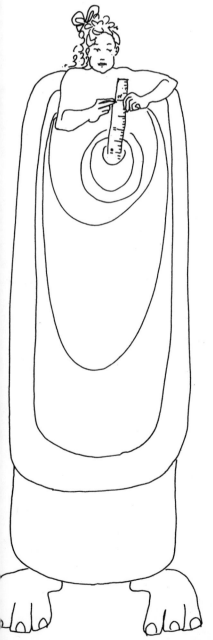

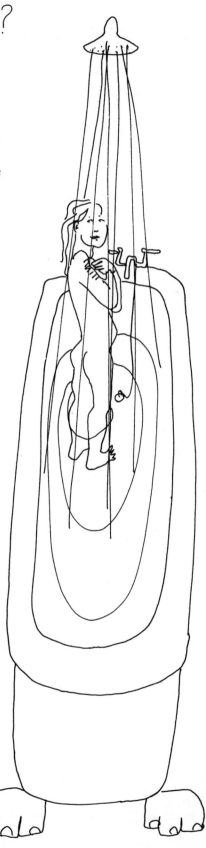

HOW TO DO IT

Ecology Check-up

It isn't easy to change the way you do things, or the way your family does them. Families don't always act the way you want them to, or the way books say they will.

One way to change habits is to pick a change that's easy for you, that you don't mind doing. An easy change makes a good start.

Try using this ecology check-list on yourself, on your family and your friends. (The publisher of this book gives you permission to make as many copies of the check-list as you want.) Some of the things

on it may not even apply to you. Just skip them. Begin by checking anything that you think goes in the "Sure—I'll Do It" column. After that, you may find you can move on to the next column, and the next.

Compare your check-list with other people's. Where do you stand? Try doing the check-list again in a month. Have you changed?

Remember, changing to even one good ecology habit is a start. And it is a good idea to try changing your own ecology habits before you go to work on projects with other people.

I can't	I don't want to	I might	I'll do it sometimes	Easy I'll do it	
					walk instead of asking for a ride
					ride a bike instead of asking for a ride
					help to organize car pools
					ask drivers to use non-lead gas
					throw papers in trash cans
					use dishes instead of paper plates; re-useable cups instead of paper cups
					save newspapers for recycling
					use the back of writing and drawing paper
					save envelopes and wrapping paper to use again
					ask your school to buy recycled paper
					save cans and bottles for recycling
					use plastic bags over and over
					avoid buying things in plastic containers or wrappers
					turn off all water faucets tightly
					fix drips and leaks
					don't let water keep running when you brush your teeth
					run dishwashers and washing machines only with full loads
					don't use the toilet as a wastebasket
					turn off lights when you're not using them
					put garbage into a compost pile
					plant trees
					fix things instead of throwing them out
					save parts from old bikes to fix new ones
					give outgrown clothes to someone smaller
					share books, games, magazines with your friends
					talk to people about ecology
					add things to this list and make copies for other people

Writing Letters in your own Town

Mr. James Short, President
American Products Company
Middletown, Kansas

Dear Mr. Short:

When you write letters to
people in your town, be sure
to have the facts right. Be
sure the letter is clear, and
easy to read.

I am a boy who lives on Oak Street
in Middletown. Every day at 9 a.m.
and 6 p.m. the American Products
whistle goes off. It makes a really
terrible noise. The dishes rattle
around on our kitchen shelves and
my baby sister cries. My ears hurt
afterwards for about five minutes.
I am writing to ask if you know how
bad the whistle is, and if there is
something you can do about it. Please
answer this letter. Thank you.

Typing is good.
Clear handwriting ———
is o.k.

Send copies of your letter
to several people who can
help you.

Sincerely,

Andrew Barbetto

Andrew Barbetto

cc means you have
sent a carbon of ———
your letter.

cc:Middletown Environmental Council

If one letter doesn't get
results, try another.

Ms. Susan Greening, Mayor
Middletown, Kansas

Dear Ms. Greening:

I am writing to ask if I can come to the Middletown
City Council meeting and complain about the American
Products whistle.

I complained to the President of American Products, but
he says he can't do anything about the whistle. Then I
measured the whistle's noise with Mr. Anthony Berg of
Middletown Environmental Council. Near my house the
whistle is 120 decibels, and I know from studying noise
pollution in my school that a noise that loud can hurt
you and maybe make you deaf. I don't want to be deaf.

Use facts ———

Please tell me if I can come to a City Council meeting.
I can bring the material about noise pollution that we
have in my class at school. I hope to hear from you.

Be polite ———————

Sincerely,

Andrew Barbetto

It's a good idea to send
a copy to the newspaper.———

cc: Mr. Anthony Berg
     The Middletown News
     Mr. James Short

Keep writing

Writing Letters to Washington

You can write a letter to anyone in the government in Washington.

If you write to the President, he will probably not see your letter, but someone on his staff will answer for him.

If you write to members of Congress, they will probably read your letter and write back.

The President's address is:
    The President of the United States
    The White House
    1600 Pennsylvania Ave. N.W.
    Washington, D.C. 20500

You can write to your Senator at:
    The U.S. Senate
    Washington, D. C. 20510

You can write to your Representative at:
    The U.S. House of Representatives
    Washington, D. C. 20515

To find the name of your Senator or Representative, call the library in your town and ask.

Mr. William Johnston
U.S. House of Representatives
Washington, D.C. 20515

Dear Mr. Johnston,

I am writing to ask you to vote against the Mile High Ski development. Because if a ski development starts in Northern National Park, there will soon be roads, and people and cars all over the park, and all the wildlife in it will be gone.

I love the park and I don't want all the beautiful forests to be cut down just so some people can ski. I think everybody should be able to see a natural park and not have it spoiled with hot dog stands and all those things that don't belong in Northern Park at all.

                    Sincerely
                    Anne McGraw
                    (age 11) ———

Tell your age. People like to be nice to children, and often answer them. Most children live with adults who vote, and congressmen know this.

Ms. Anne McGraw
1672 State Street
Lincoln, Idaho

Dear Ms. McGraw:

Thank you for your letter concerning the development of the Mile High ski and vacation resort in Northern National Park near your home. I am glad to have your views on this matter. You can be sure I will consider them before I vote on the "Recreational Developments and National Parks" Bill.

Sincerely,

Wm. Johnston
Congressman, Sixth District

Be careful of letters like this! They don't mean much. The Congressman does not say how he will vote.

He probably does not agree.

A letter-writing campaign from your friends and your friends' parents, might help him change his mind.

Making a Tape Recording

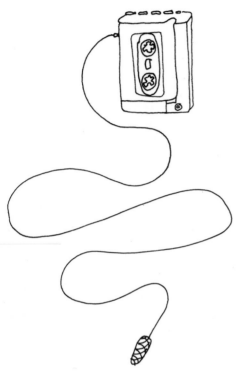

You can use a tape recording in many ways:
for a radio broadcast,
to play for your class in school,
to prove something in a public meeting,
to send to someone whose help you need on a project.
When you play an interesting recording, people listen.

"This is Diane Blackman.
I'm interviewing Mrs. Martha
Stewart, the very first person
to throw trash into the new
litter basket at the corner
of Dewey and Sparkman streets.
Mrs. Stewart, what made
you throw that milkshake
container into the basket?"

"We're standing in the middle
of Ellis Field at ten o'clock
in the morning of a warm
sunny day in September, 1973.
We are Jerry Rosen, Amy Dana,
and Jack Innis The sounds
you will hear are us, moving
around and talking, then
some bird songs and insect
noises and the sound of the
wind blowing through the
grass. This is the way the
country sounds."

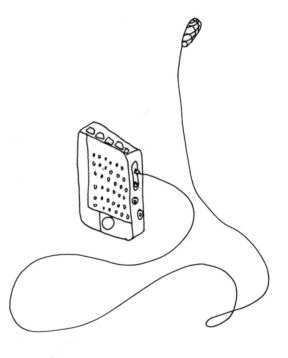

"We're in the office of Mr. Arnold Pillman, the president of Tru-Color Paints. We have a list of questions to ask him that our class made up, and the first one is, 'Do you know that the Alabama River outside your factory sometimes turns red or white or purple when you are making paint?'"

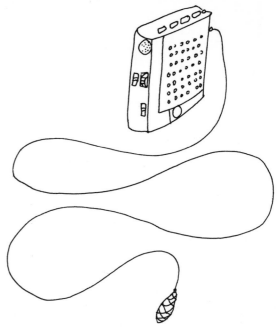

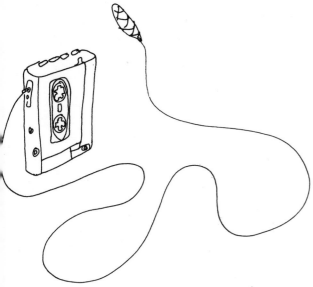

"This is Bob Waterman. I am standing outside my house at 137 Elm Street. A jet plane is coming nearer and nearer. The sound you hear is the jet plane right over my house at 2:29 p.m."

"This is Joy and Robert and Suzanne, standing across the street from the Plainfield School. The sounds you hear are construction noises from the new office building that is going up on this corner. Imagine how you would like to do schoolwork across the street from this much noise."

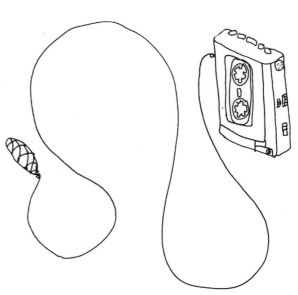

81

Writing a Newspaper Story

A newspaper story is good because many people see it. Some papers will send their own reporters, and some will use your news stories. For the newspaper, all facts must be checked. The story should be typed. A morning newspaper needs your story in the afternoon of the day before. An afternoon paper needs your story early in the morning.

Put your name
and phone number
here

Don't write a headline - the paper will.
Leave space for it.

Tell - who
    when
    where
    did what
in the first paragraph

Explain why in
the next paragraphs

    Members of the third grade class of Lincoln School got up early this morning, October 13, and met at the corner of Park and Summer Streets, where they began to record the amount of traffic that passed the corner between 7:30 and 9.

    As lookouts called out "car" or "school bus", some recorders wrote down the count in notebooks. Other recorders counted the number of children who crossed the street when the lights turned.

    When all their information is organized, the third graders plan to make a report to their school assembly, the PTA, the traffic police and the Town Council. They hope to have their busiest school corner closed to all traffic except bicycles as a result of their report.

More ⟵ write "more" on a continued news story.

The traffic project was started by
Alice Johnson, 8, who lives on nearby
Autumn Drive. Alice thinks that children
at Lincoln School need more safety and
quiet. "I can hardly get across the street
to my school, because I have to wait so long
for the light to change. And then I'm afraid
the cars won't wait for me," Alice said.
"And the sound of the traffic is so bad all
day long that we can hardly hear each other   —— Use people's
when we're trying to work in school."   real words

Sam Southwaite, 9, of Pine Tree Lane,
agrees with Alice. He has made a map to
show that all the traffic now using Park
Street could be turned off onto Gilbert
Avenue instead.

James Bergen, the third grade teacher,
says that the traffic survey is part of his
class's study of ecology. "We are learning,"
he says, "how many problems of ecology are
connected. In this project we see the results
of air pollution and noise pollution, as well
as the safety problems that result when town
developments are built without adequate plan-
ning. We hope to call the attention of this
town to the traffic mess around our school -
and we want to get some direct action."

All the third graders agree with
their teacher. They have decided to stick
with their project until the Town Council
comes to a decision one way or another on
their plan. They believe that the decision
must be in their favor. "All I want," says
Alice Johnson, "is to be able to ride my
bike to school and be safe."

30 #   ←——————— Either one of these signs means
                              the end.

Starting a Block Association

Block associations start when somebody says:

"Let's have a block association."
You could be that somebody, along with an adult. You will need to talk to lots of people on your block. If people want to work together, call a meeting. Maybe they could meet at your house.

At the first meeting, people could tell each other their wishes for the block, and decide which ones to work on.

If a whole block association asks the city for something, like quieter trash cans, or a speed limit for cars on the street, the city is more likely to agree. You can make your block a better place to live.

84

Working for Ecology on the Street

If you want people to listen to you, you will have to go where they are.

Take a survey . . .

"We're taking a neighborhood survey. Would you be interested in working for a children's playground on the lot at the corner?"

Put notices in people's mailboxes . . .

Picket a polluter...

Ask people to sign petitions...

Holding A Press Conference

A press conference lets you tell your news to television and radio stations and the newspapers. A press conference is only for important news. When school children do something exciting and helpful in the community, most people think it is news, so they are likely to pay attention to you.

Class 6B of Street School made a study of air pollution in their town. They decided to give an award — "The Polluter Prize" — to the three worst polluters they found. They planned a press conference so everyone would know about their work.

They picked a day to invite their parents, other people in their school, and the press: two newspapers, a radio station and a television station.

They telephoned the newspapers and the radio and television stations, and asked for the city editors. They told the city editors about their study and the "Polluter Prize" and made sure they wrote down the date and time and place.

On the day of the press conference, some people were at the door to greet guests, and others stood by the display to explain it. There was a one-page report of the project for everyone who came.

Then, Robert Brown asked everyone to sit down while he awarded the "Polluter Prizes."

One of the polluters came in person to get his prize! He was Mr. Dan Arbiter of the Green Valley Foundry. Mr. Arbiter said he was working to cut down pollution by his factory. He thanked Class 6B for their concern with pollution.

That night, Class 6B's press conference was news on television and on the radio. The next morning, the class made the front page of the newspapers. The day after that, the Mayor announced big fines for polluters. Class 6B's work had worked!

Ecology Organizations

Environmental Action Coalition, Inc.
235 East 49th Street
New York, New York 10017

The Fund For Animals
140 West 57th Street
New York, New York 10019

Friends of the Earth
529 Commercial Street
San Francisco, California 94111

Zero Population Growth
4080 Fabian Way
Palo Alto, California 94303

Massachusetts Audubon Society
Lincoln, Mass. 01773

National Wildlife Federation
1412 16th Street, N.W.
Washington, D.C. 20036

National Audubon Society, Inc.
950 Third Avenue
New York, New York 10022

Sierra Club
1050 Mills Tower
San Francisco, California 94104

These are some of the organizations that can help you find out about environmental laws and agencies in your town or your state. They can help you find the organizations near you. They can tell you where to go for information, and where to take information of your own in order to get action. If there is no branch of one of these organizations listed in your phone book, write to the address above to find the office nearest you.

The federal government agency concerned with all environmental problems in the United States is the Environmental Protection Agency, Waterside Mall, 401 M Street, S.W., Washington, D.C. 20460.

All of these organizations will send you materials about ecology. Many business organizations and industries also send out advertisements and booklets about ecological problems. Look for advertisements of their materials in magazines. Of course, most business groups want you to think that their answer to a problem is the right one, or that their product is good for the environment. This may be true, or it may not.

To decide for yourself, compare the materials that ecology groups send you with those from business organizations. The more you read, the more you will see that there are no easy answers to ecological problems and that you will have to work out some of the answers for yourself. That is a part of the complicated work of saving the earth.

Reading About Ecology

About Ecology

Only One Earth. By Barbara Ward and René Dubos. New York: Norton, 1972.
   A report about the world's environment written for the United Nations.

The Closing Circle. By Barry Commoner. New York: Knopf, 1971; Bantam, 1972.
   A book about the connections and cycles of life on earth.

The Only Earth We Have. By Lawrence Pringle. New York: Macmillan, 1969.
   A clear statement of the problems of ecology. A book for children.

The Web of Life. By John H. Storer. New York: Signet, 1968.
   The relationship of living things to each other and to the environment.

Understanding Ecology. By Elizabeth T. Billington. New York: Warne, 1968.
   An introduction to the science of ecology. A book for children.

About Ecology Action

Defending the Environment. By Joseph L. Sax. New York: Knopf, 1971; Vintage Books, 1972.
   A handbook for citizen action.

Earth Tool Kit. Edited by Sam Love. New York: Pocket Books, 1971.
   A book about working for ecology. Lists ecology agencies and organizations in every state.

Improve Your Environment: Fight Pollution with Pictures. AC-26. Eastman Kodak Co., Rochester,
   New York 14650. How to take photographs that show environmental problems and
   neighborhood action.

Science Projects in Ecology. By Seymour Simon. New York: Holiday House, 1972.
   Projects that demonstrate how the environment operates. A book for children.

Reference Books

The Complete Ecology Fact Book. Edited by Philip Nobile and John Deedy.
   New York: Doubleday/Anchor, 1972. A handbook of statistics about ecology.

World Facts and Trends. By John McHale. New York: Collier Books, 1972.
   Ecological facts, tables and graphs presented in terms of the whole earth.

Newsletters

Eco-News. Published by EAC (Environmental Action Coalition), 235 East 49th Street, New York, N.Y.
   10017. An interesting, practical newsletter about ecology for city children.

Ranger Rick's Nature Magazine. Published by National Wildlife Federation, 1412 16th St., N.W.,
   Washington, D.C. 20036. A magazine with many color pictures about ecology.

The "So You" Series. Brochures published especially for young people by
The Fund for Animals, 140 West 57th Street, New York, N.Y. 10019·

The Young Naturalist. Published by Massachusetts Audubon Society, Lincoln, Mass., 01773.
   A magazine about the natural world.

People everywhere
breathe the same air,
share the same seas,
live together on the land.
People everywhere
who learn, plan,
work, care,
can
save the earth.

Index

Photo Credits

"Bound to Get Clear Water" by permission of the *Clearwater* crew.

Typewriter art by Darryle Johnson.

About the Author

Betty Miles believes people should take action on the things they care about. This book grew out of that conviction.

As a teacher at Bank Street College of Education she is concerned with the connection between children's reading and their concept formation, values and actions. Her books for children, among them JUST THINK!, A HOUSE FOR EVERYONE, and WHAT IS THE WORLD?, relate to this concern.

Betty Miles is active in a group working for greater honesty in the portrayal of women and girls in all books for children. She has also written many magazine articles on children and education and has worked on several educational films.

She lives with her family in Rockland County, New York.

About the Artist

Claire A. Nivola is a painter and sculptor whose work has been both exhibited and reproduced. She illustrated her first book for children, *The Disobedient Eels* (Pantheon), in 1970, the year she graduated from Radcliffe College. Since that time she has worked as a graphic designer and consultant, an art director of a magazine, and an instructor in graphic design with an urban education program in Boston.

She lives in Cambridge, Massachusetts where she is now pursuing her own work as an artist.